From the desktop of Jeffrey Simmons

A vacation in Paris inspired Miroslav Sasek to create childrens travel guides to the big cities of the world. He brought me *This is Paris* in 1958 when I was publishing in London, and we soon followed up with *This is London*. Both books were enormously successful, and his simple vision grew to include more than a dozen books. Their amusing text, coupled with bright and charming illustrations, made for a series unlike any other, and garnered Sasek (as we always called him) the international and popular acclaim he deserved.

I was thrilled to learn that *This is the Way to the Moon* (originally called *This is Cape Canaveral* and then changed to *This is Cape Kennedy* in 1964) will once again find its rightful place on bookshelves. Sasek is no longer with us (and I have lost all contact with his family), but I am sure he would be delighted to know that a whole new generation of wide-eyed readers is being introduced to his whimsical, imaginative, and enchanting world.

Your name here

M · Sasek

THIS
IS
THE WAY TO
THE MOON

Published by arrangement with Simon & Schuster Books for Young Readers,
Simon & Schuster Children's Publishing Division

This edition first published in the United States of America in 2009 by
UNIVERSE PUBLISHING
A Division of Rizzoli International Publications, Inc.
300 Park Avenue South
New York, NY 10010
www.rizzoliusa.com

Text and pictures copyright © Miroslav Sasek, 1963, 1964

Originally published as *This is Cape Canaveral* (1963); last published as *This is Cape Kennedy* (1964)

Cover, page 3, and page 5 type and illustrations on pages 61-64 by Jessie Hartland

*See updated Moon facts at end of book

2015   2016   2017   /   13 12 11 10 9

Printed in China

ISBN–13: 978-0-7893-1842-8

Library of Congress Control Number: 2008911177

Cover design: Sara E. Stemen

THIS
IS
THE WAY TO
THE MOON

To reflect the official return of the geographical name Cape Canaveral (from Cape Kennedy), in 1973, all text has been changed accordingly.

UNIVERSE

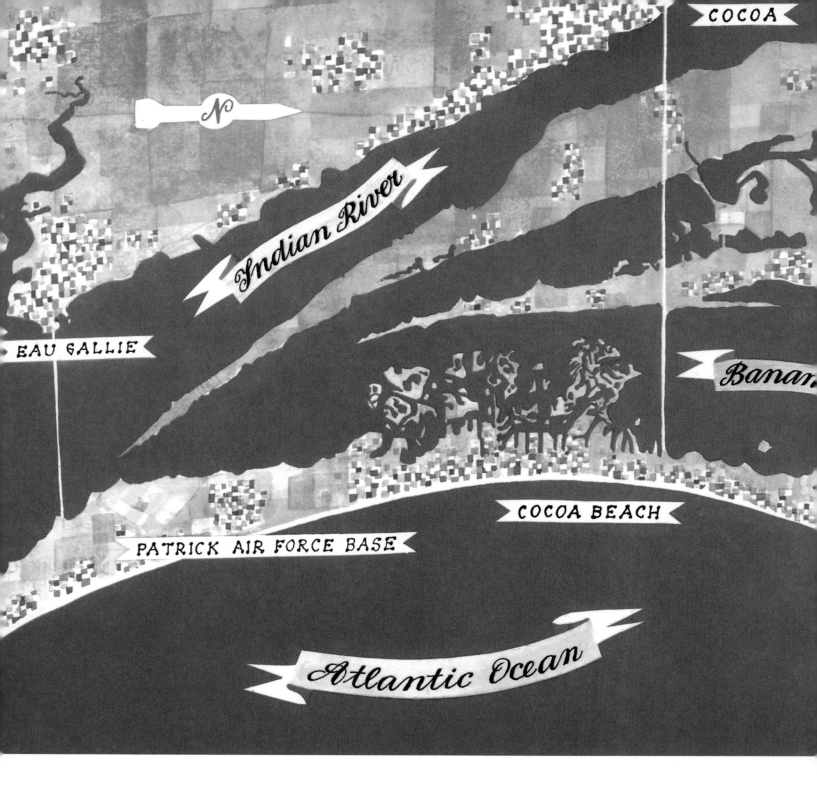

On the east coast of Florida, 212 miles north of Miami, you enter a land of giants, of science-fiction-turned-fact, among whose denizens are the Atlas, the Thor, the Saturn, the Polaris, the Redstone, the Titan, the Jupiter. This is the land of satellites, space vehicles and spacemen, "Space Capital of the World," "Gateway to the Moon," "U.S. Spaceport No. One"—Cape Canaveral.*

At Cape Canaveral the effective speed limit is 17,400 m.p.h.

A few miles away it is somewhat less.

Here you are invited to have "Fun in the sun."

But one day in the sun can get you sixty days in the shade.

When this quiet beach is filled with crowds staring north, one knows that something historic is happening at Cape Canaveral four miles away.

But even at ordinary times one feels the nearness of the Cape.

A sticker for your car—

a card for your friend—

the photo shop—

a silver souvenir—

MISSILE CHARMS

by Mini-Missile

the church.

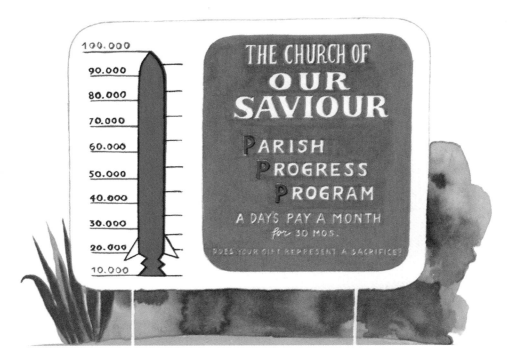

THE CHURCH OF
OUR
SAVIOUR
PARISH
PROGRESS
PROGRAM
A DAYS PAY A MONTH
for 30 MOS.
DOES YOUR GIFT REPRESENT A SACRIFICE?

Here they make doors
into portals and space-folk
from small mortals.

Missile REALTY

COCOA BEACH
FLA.

SU 3-7661

WEZY
MOBIL NEWS

Missiles, missiles everywhere—

WHITE CAPS
STEAK
HOUSE

EAT

Missile Taxi

117 COCOA AV

SU 3-7276

15

and earthly space to let.

"Toast of the Coast in Our Orbit Room."

"Space flight is Missile Business.
Motel Space is Our Business."

Cape Colony Inn. Some day in this motel there may be
a plaque saying: "Here lived the first U.S. astronauts."*

In the lobby there stood the model of an Atlas.
The ancient Atlas carried the world on his shoulders;
the modern one carried the first American into orbit.

The only place on the Cape where you can see real missiles at close range is the permanent display in front of the Technical Laboratory at Patrick Air Force Base.

Inside this building are stored thousands of miles of magnetic tape and film, recording all the data from Cape Canaveral flights.

At Patrick Air Force Base is the headquarters of the Air Force Missile Task Center, which operates a dozen stations belonging to the Atlantic Missile Range. This missile test range extends some 10,000 miles over the sea, all the way to the Indian Ocean.

A leaflet says: "The display lends itself especially well to family photography." This man finds it a bit hard.

US NAVY
POLARIS

LENGTH   28 Feet
DIAMETER 54 Inches
WEIGHT   30.000 Pounds
RANGE   1.200 Nau-mi

US ARMY
PERSHING

HEIGHT: 34 Feet
RANGE: Selective
SPEED: Supersonic
PROPULSION:
  Two-stage solid
       propellant
WARHEAD: Nuclear

To the tourist these may be missiles. In the missileman's slang, they are called "birds."

Cocoa Beach used to be a small village. In only ten years it grew at space speed from 273 inhabitants to over 7,000. Cape Canaveral is next door.*

But its door is not too easy to open.

Gateway to U.S. Spaceport No. One, the Missile Test Annex.

Through these portals indeed pass daily only missilemen; the 13,500 scientists, engineers and technicians who work here for the Navy, the Army, the Air Force and NASA (National Aeronautics and Space Administration).

The first missile was launched from here on July 24, 1950. Since then, over 3,000 space vehicles of all shapes, types, and sizes have been fired from the Cape.

This is all there was on the
Cape some years ago.

Today nearby there grow forests of antennae, which track missiles in flight. Some look like vast celestial combs—

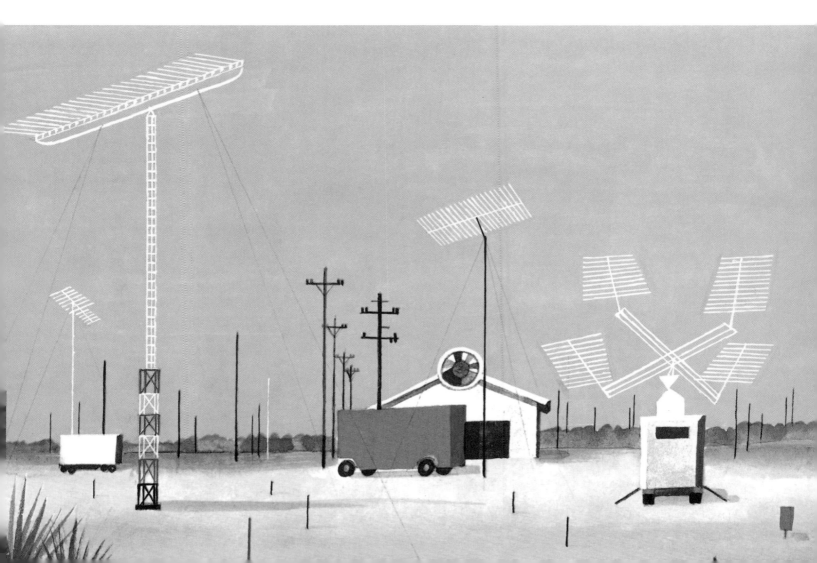

Here is a radar that tracks the missile just for a short while; 90 seconds after launching, a similar radar in the Islands of the Bahamas takes over.

some like huge spider webs. This antenna is called the "Dish."

The fuel makes up about nine-tenths of the weight of each rocket. Most common is a mixture of RP-1 (something like kerosene) with liquid oxygen (LOX).

Safety facilities for those handling another of the liquid fuels.

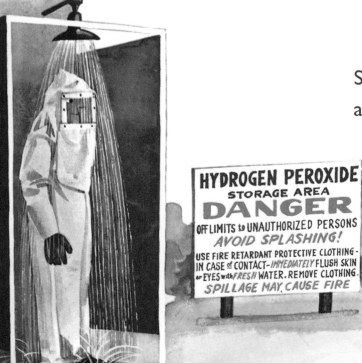

The process of fueling is dangerous and is done only just before launching, as with this Vanguard.*

The U.S. Air Force Minuteman was the first American missile propelled by solid fuel.

The Minuteman can be launched from an underground silo—

the U.S. Navy Polaris A-1, from a
submerged submarine—

the U.S. Army Pershing, from a
mobile erector–launcher.*

Titan

height—100 feet

weight—110 tons, of which 100 tons represent fuel

thrust—300,000 pounds, equivalent to 4,500,000 h.p., or the combined power of 15,300 average-size cars

Rocket—spotters please note: this is a later development of the Titan shown on pages 21 and 22.*

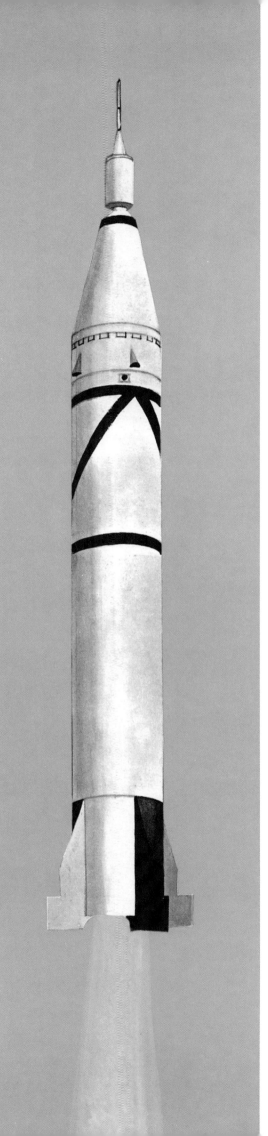

Jupiter-C

On January 31, 1958 this missile launched Explorer I, the first U.S. scientific satellite.*

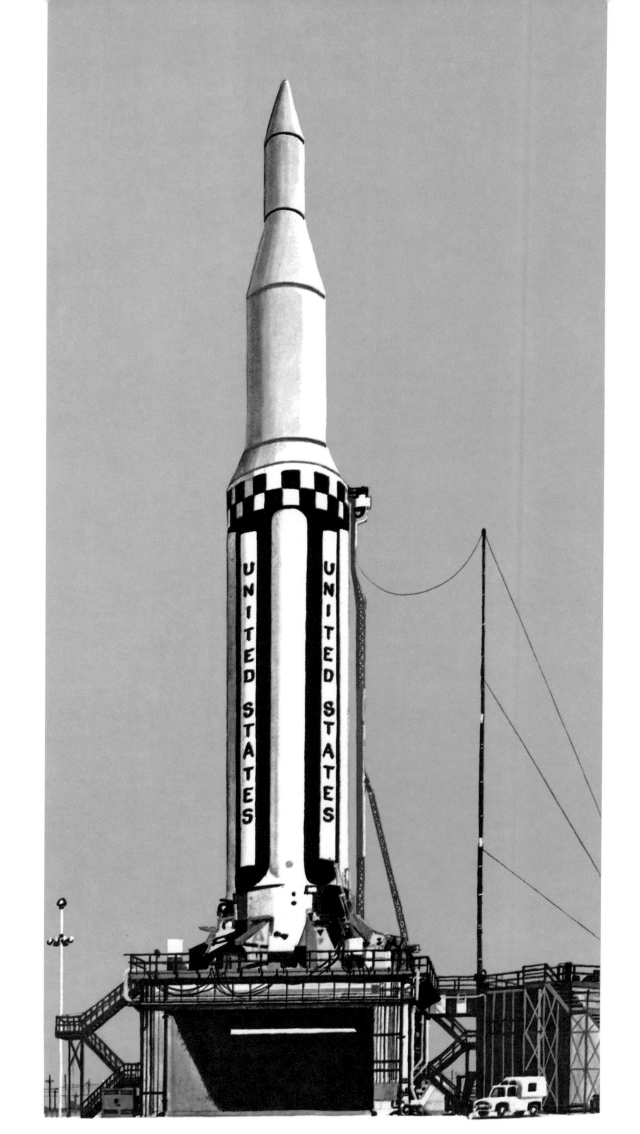

The NASA Saturn—the largest known rocket.

Its first stage, a cluster of eight Jupiter engines, is 21 feet in diameter.
Its height is 163 feet, and its thrust equals 32,000,000 horsepower.
This is the missile that is aiming for the moon.

It was built at Huntsville in Alabama and was transported
to the Cape by Saturn barges—

and to the launch site by special trucks.

Mercury Redstone

height—83 feet
weight—33 tons

On January 31, 1961, this missile propelled
a 37–pound astronaut named Mr. Ham 422
miles down the Atlantic Missile Range.

On May 5, 1961 another Mercury Redstone propelled a rather heavier
astronaut named Alan Shepard, Jr. 303 miles down the range, making him
the first American spaceman. His 16-minute flight was the result of years of
preparation and cost around $400,000,000.*

He is carrying his air conditioner. His space suit is a bit more expensive
than Mr. Ham's. It is made to measure, consists of 1,300 parts, and weighs
22-pounds. Its cost—$2,000.

The National Aeronautics and Space Administration Project
Mercury Astronauts, the first seven U.S. space pioneers.

NASA, a civilian organization, was created in 1958 by an act of Congress. Its overall plans include experiments in physics, chemistry, astronomy, astrophysics, and several space projects of which the first was Project Mercury. The aim of Project Mercury: to put man into orbit and to investigate his ability to perform in space.*

All the manned orbital flights have been made by Mercury-Atlas. Atlas is built in San Diego, California, and is flown to Cape Canaveral by special aircraft.

Each type of missile has a special launch complex. This one is for the Atlas.

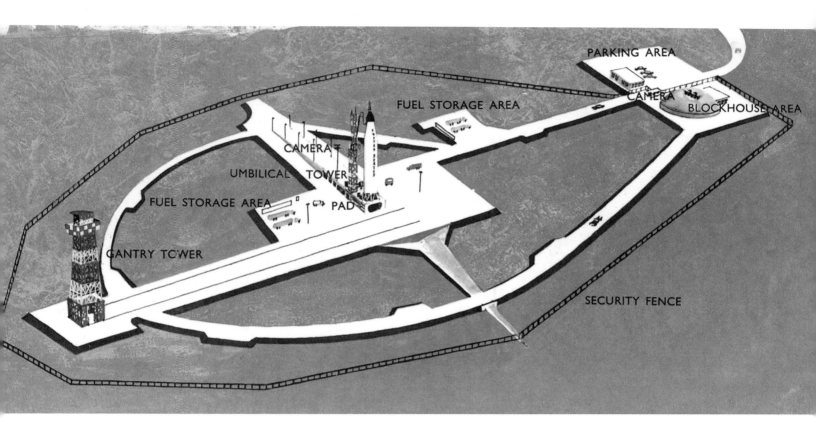

The gantry is a service tower from which the rocket is checked and made ready for lift-off. Before the launching this vast, many-tiered platform rumbles away on its rails to its parking area.

The umbilical tower keeps the missile "alive" on its pad just prior to flight.

The blockhouse is a reinforced concrete bunker from which the firing of the missile is directed.

Everybody entering the launching area must wear a helmet.

45

Mercury Atlas with its spacecraft during pre-launch checkouts:

height—93 feet
weight—264,000 pounds, including 235,000 pounds of fuel
thrust—360,000 pounds
speed—17,526 m.p.h. (at maximum velocity)

The red device on top of the spacecraft is the escape tower. It is provided with a powerful rocket, which in case something should go wrong before launching, could lift the capsule off the Atlas and parachute the astronaut safely down. After a successful launching, this tower drops off at an altitude of about 50 miles and burns up.

Now the gantry tower has been moved away and the astronaut is quite alone in his capsule. His last connection with earth before his flight into space is the cord of the umbilical tower and the voice from the control room during the final stages of the countdown.

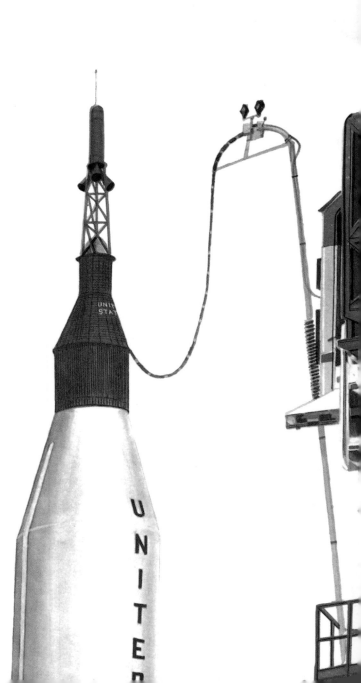

That voice comes from the blockhouse.

This is how the control room looks during the count-down. There are no windows here at all. Engineers and technicians can watch the rocket only on TV screens or by periscope.

The big bird lifts off.

During the first minute of its flight the Atlas consumes more fuel than a jet airliner during a flight from New York to London.

Now begins the astronaut's lonely journey into space.

"Birdwatchers" at the Cape's press site. Thousands of others, usually less well equipped, crowd Cocoa Beach, and millions more throughout the country do their bird-watching by television.

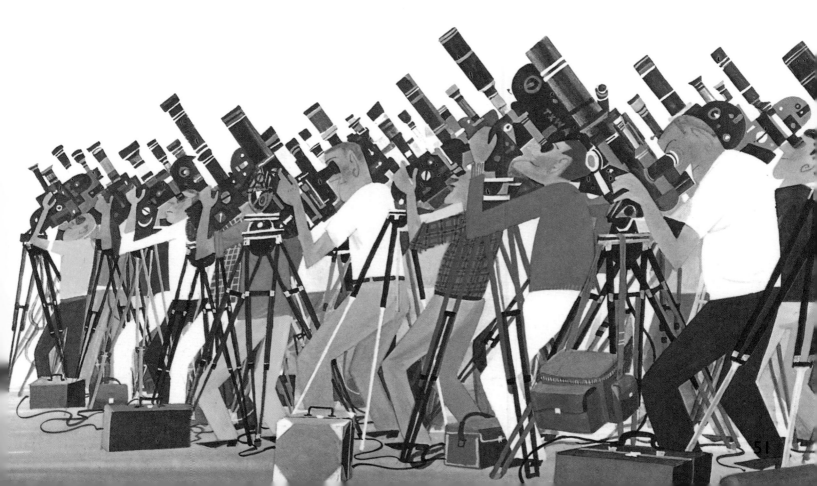

The Mercury Atlas spacecraft looks like a television tube, and is made like a thermos bottle so as to keep cool inside. It is 10 feet high, 6 feet in diameter, and weighs one ton.

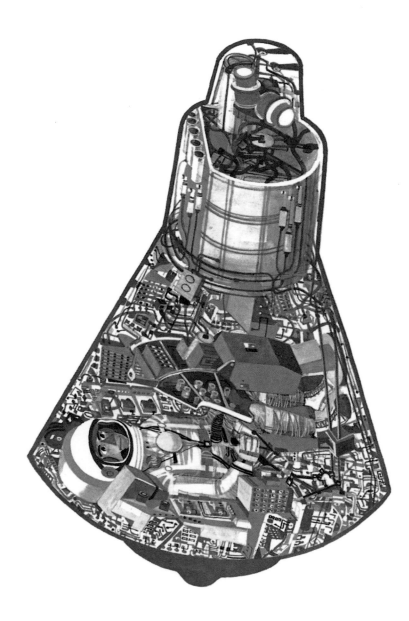

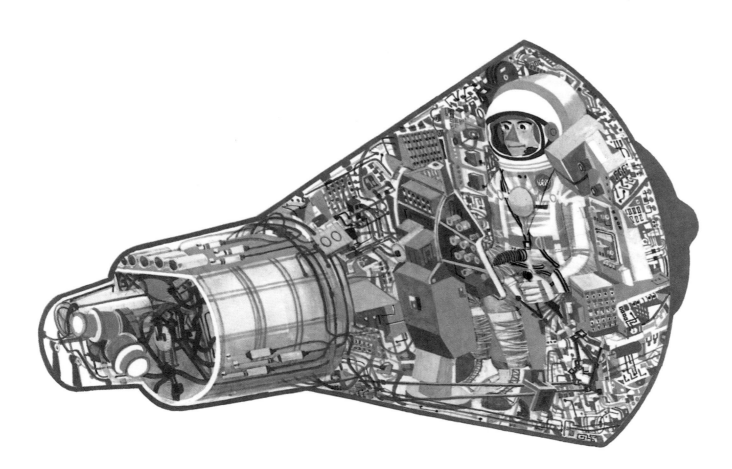

The capsule separates from the Atlas at an altitude of 100 miles and is turned by small rockets to fly with the broad heat-shield forward. At that moment its speed is 17,400 m.p.h. To complete one orbit of the earth takes 90 minutes. Each orbit carries the astronaut through the full cycle of day and night.

Immediately after the launching of the Atlas, Mercury Control Center, a couple of miles away, takes over from the blockhouse and becomes the brain of the entire mission. With the help of the tracking stations all over the world, these men have complete control over every detail of the flight: the capsule and the condition of the astronaut up to his re-entry into the atmosphere, and the recovery of the man and his spacecraft. *

All tracking stations and key information from them are displayed on this World Map:

CTN	Canton Island	CK	Cape Kennedy	ZZB	Zanzibar
HAW	Kauai, Hawaii	BDA	Bermuda	IOS	Indian Ocean Ship
CAL	Point Arguello, California	ATS	Atlantic Ocean Ship	MUC	Muchea, Australia
GYM	Guaymas, Mexico	CYI	Canary Islands	WOM	Woomera, Australia
TEX	Corpus Christi, Texas	KNO	Kano, Nigeria		

40,000 people worked on Project Mercury. Of these, 15,000 were engaged on the recovery, using thirty ships and hundreds of aircraft.

Next morning, Cape Canaveral became a household name in every language.

The astronaut has fulfilled his mission and put on his civilian clothes again. After the big official receptions in Washington and New York, little Cocoa Beach also welcomes its hero.

And two local specialists in confectionary construction build him a chocolate spacecraft. Many of the same people who worked so hard to preserve the original capsule will happily help to destroy this one.

Then for a while the beach again becomes quiet and sleepy. There is nothing happening.

Or is there? A tiny tourist from Manhattan is about to fly to Moonhattan.

Here are some facts about our space program TODAY!

Page 7:
On November 29, 1963, the Launch Operations Center and the Cape Canaveral Auxiliary Air Force Station were renamed the John F. Kennedy Space Center in memory of the assassinated president. The following month the name of NASA's facility there was also changed to honor the president, and in 1964 the U.S. Board of Geographical Names changed the name of the geographical cape from Cape Canaveral to Cape Kennedy. The new geographical name lasted only until 1973, when local residents petitioned the Board to officially recognize the original name, Cape Canaveral, which had been the moniker used for the region for over 400 years.

Page 18:
In 1962, the original seven astronauts invested in a motel, which was then called the Cape Colony Inn. Today, a hotel chain has replaced the original motel. There is no plaque. But, there is a sign outside the motel which lists the names of the original seven and their missions. The sign has been there for about ten years.

Page 24:
The city of Cocoa Beach was established on June 5, 1925. There was a 1000% population increase there during the decade between 1950 and 1960.

Page 33:
A solid rocket or a solid-fuel rocket is a rocket with a motor that uses solid propellants (a combination of fuel and oxidizer). Now, liquid and hybrid rockets offer more fuel efficient and controllable alternatives. Solid rockets are still used today, although less frequently.

Page 35:
The Polaris was replaced in the U.S. Navy by the Poseidon in 1972. In the 1980s, both were replaced by Trident I.

Page 36:
Titan was a family of expendable U.S. rockets used between 1959 and 2005. A total of 368 rockets of this family were launched. The final Titan rocket was launched from Vandenberg Air Force Base in California in 2005.

Page 37:
Explorer I was officially known as Satellite 1958 Alpha. Explorer I was the first of the long-running Explorer program, which, as of April 2007, has launched ninety Explorer probes.

Page 41:
Alan Shepard, Jr. was launched in a Mercury space-craft named Freedom 7 atop a Redstone rocket. After extensive preparations and several frustrating launch attempts, he became the first American to make a space flight. Although the rocket didn't have enough thrust to place him into earth's orbit, the Mercury spacecraft did reach space, thus making him the first American in space. His Freedom 7 capsule reached an altitude of 116 miles during the suborbital flight and splashed down some 304 miles into the Atlantic.

Page 43:
The NASA was established fifty years ago; it began operations on October 1, 1958 with a staff of eighty spread among four labs. Today, NASA consists of fifteen facilities and employs more than 17,000 people.

Page 54:
The Mercury Control Center, where NASA directed the flights of unmanned and manned space capsules from 1960-65, is no longer in use.

MORE

On July 20, 1969, Commander Neil Armstrong of Apollo 11 became the first person to step onto the moon. "Buzz" Aldrin joined him a moment later.

Armstrong said the historic words, "One small step for man, one giant leap for mankind."

They scooped up 44 lbs of lunar rocks to bring back for scientific research.

Four days later the lunar module with the three astronauts reentered the atmosphere...

MORE

...and "splashed down" as planned, in the Pacific Ocean.

In August a ticker tape parade was held for the astronauts along New York City's "Canyon of Heroes."

John F. Kennedy's dream had come true—

man had walked on the moon!